SHAPE SHiFTER

*A Minidoka
Concentration Camp Legacy*

POEMS

by

LAWRENCE MATSUDA

ENDICOTT
and HUGH
BOOKS

Endicott and Hugh Books
PO Box 13305
Burton, WA 98013
www.endicottandhughbooks.com

SHAPE SHIFTER: A Minidoka Concentration Camp Legacy

Front cover: "Kabuki Play" lithograph © 1985 Roger Shimomura
Back cover: "Portrait of Lawrence Matsuda" © 2015 Alfred Arreguin
Book design and cover design Masha Shubin

ISBN: 978-0-9993646-8-0 Trade paperback

Printed in the United States of America

1 3 5 7 9 10 8 6 4 2

ALSO BY LAWRENCE MATSUDA

POETRY

A Cold Wind from Idaho
Glimpses of a Forever Foreigner
Boogie Woogie Criss Cross (with Tess Gallagher)

GRAPHIC NOVEL

Fighting for America: Nisei Soldiers

HISTORIC NOVEL

My Name Is Not Viola

Praise for Lawrence Matsuda's

SHAPE SHIFTER:
A Minidoka Concentration Camp Legacy

Larry Matsuda is a compelling storyteller. In "Shape Shifter", a book of poetry, he meanders through his life with recollections, reflections and introspection and the reader hurries along with him to the next poem - through Seattle before and after life in the Minidoka ID Concentration Camp, to Japan, on a fishing boat and across this country. The reader is forced to hang on to every word, sometimes wiping away a tear; sometimes laughing out loud. A beautiful collection of poetry telling the story of a life well lived.

> Dorothy Holland Mann, author of *Guide My Feet, a Memoir*

Matsuda summons us to imagine the unbearable and the possible. His poems reveal the truth of our humanity by illuminating a life of heartbreak, authenticity, and candor.

> Tilman Smith, Co-author with Ilsa Govan, *What's Up with White Women? Unpacking Sexism and White Privilege in Pursuit of Racial Justice*

We need shapeshifters like Matsuda to keep reviving the pain-valleys and corrosive denials of Minidoka, the WWII concentration camp in Idaho where he was born. Matsuda takes on the now absent forms of his family members who, like him, had to withstand the insidious and spiritually annihilating betrayals of their government's lies, accusations, ultimate soul-sickening erasures of identity. When your jailors doze your burial grounds, you have the right to howl.

> Tess Gallagher, author of *Is, Is Not.*

Larry Matsuda beautifully and sorrowfully captures the deep and painful emotions suffered by Japanese Americans who endured an unconstitutional mass incarceration during WWII. Delving into the raw scars of survivors and descendants, Matsuda brings the reader closer to understanding the impact injustices have on individuals, families, communities, and our greater society.

Robyn Achilles, *Executive Director Friends of Minidoka*.

CONTENTS

IV.

V.

VI.

VII.

Lawrence Matsuda's poems in *Shape Shifter: A Minidoka Concentration Camp Legacy* express the reverberating trauma of his family's imprisonment in the Minidoka Concentration Camp during WWII. The Matsuda family was among 120,000 Japanese Americans who, without due process—not committing a single crime, were forced by our government into United States concentration camps at the hands of U.S. soldiers armed with bayonets. Their crime was their race.

In predominantly White America, people of color are often seen as the "other". For Asian Americans there is the ordeal of sometimes being viewed as both foreign and the enemy. (WWII, the Korean War, and the Vietnam War were all fought in Asian countries.) And Donald Trump, in blaming China for the pandemic, was the catalyst for 10,905 hate crimes against Asian Americans between March 19, 2020 and December 31, 2021 as reported in the "National Report, December 2021" by *Stop AAPI Hate.*

Matsuda's fiercely honest poems come at an important time of acute need in our multi-ethnic culture, as right-wing activists are demanding schools not be allowed to teach the racist history of the United States. It is within this larger context that his poetry gives voice to the legacy of discrimination, racism, and hate that tragically still exist today that everyone must be aware of if there is any hope of ensuring, as Martin Luther King, Jr. said, "the arc of the moral universe is long, but it bends toward justice."

For a person of color, various cultural environments require the ability to adapt in order to fit in—or to shift shape...shape shifting. In a hostile culture this ability can be a matter of survival. But there can be a cost of splitting off one's identity and adapting when powerful emotions too often are hammered down. In his long history of social activism, and in these poems, Matsuda defies the advice of the Japanese proverb, "the nail that stands out gets hammered down". In Elaine Ikoma Ko's *North American Post* interview with Lawrence Matsuda, "A Masterful Life," he points out, "Underlying many of the poems is anger. Usually, Japanese

Americans rarely speak about their incarceration and when they do, they focus on the bad living conditions, food, and loss of property. Rarely, do they discuss the emotions—anger and sense of betrayal. I go straight to those emotions in my poems."

Although the poems reflect anger and a deep sense of sadness, there are also poems that reflect Matsuda's range in a lighter shift to his whimsical and playful side, reflecting both resilience and the healing balm of humor. The playful side was no surprise when he shared the first poem he ever wrote. "When I was about seven, I wrote a poem for a contest at Safeway about Skylark bread. 'Skylark bread is the bread for me/because it gives me energy/Other breads say they are fine/but they aren't worth a dime.'"

Lawrence Matsuda's acclaimed literary journey has come a long way since Skylark bread and we are honored to publish *Shape Shifter: A Minidoka Concentration Camp Legacy*. In this, his latest book of poetry, he uses his considerable talent to create work which he describes, "demonstrates the move from being a survivor and victim of trauma, to being a witness. It is my hope that others who have suffered trauma can benefit from poems as they explore methods of their own to find peace of mind."

Jeanie Davies Okimoto
Publisher, Endicott and Hugh Books

I.

Tess asks, "At night do you run with the wolves
or pack with coyotes?"

Being two fish facing opposite directions,
I swim with King Salmon,
dodge gill nets, sea lions, and fishermen.
Night brothers know my human alter ego
hunts them during the day.
They vow to evade my hooks.

At Point Defiance a 25-pound King grabs my bait.
He sounds and surfaces with a run towards the boat.
My line falls slack. I reel madly and catch up.
He circles. I recognize his large adipose fin
and drop the net as he turns into it.
I roll him in and pull the hooks.
His eyes are not dead.

"Swim away brother," I say and lift him free.

That night we meet again near the Puyallup River.
He speaks of his three-thousand-mile journey
and urges me to remain a fish.
He doubts that I would ever make it home
or find peace as a man, unless I stop fighting WWII.

On a Model T flatbed
strapped furniture bounces,
wooden arms and legs splay,
frayed ropes crisscross
a cat's cradle over tattered canvas.

Rust eats metal floorboards,
opens new vistas to the highway below.
Medusa-haired mother,
clutches runny nose babies.
Dark eyes have no pupils,
flat breasts give no milk.

Years later, Lang photographs Dad
standing at the Block 33
canteen cash register,
his white long johns peek out
from his shirt sleeves.
Baggy khaki pants
sag over crepe soles.

Japanese mothers with crying babies
stand in line, hope for something
nourishing to keep breasts from
drying up like the Idaho desert.

Under the Block 26 machine gun nest,
Dad corrals us for a family photo.

Mom wears a scratchy maroon
sweater and checkered cotton dress.
Faded rickrack trims
her checked apron.

She balances me, a baby on her knee,
my head falls sideways.
Six-year old, Alan furrows his brow.

Before the iris shutter snaps,
Alan's bare toes protrude from
torn shoe caps.

Taut laces crisscross shiny eyelets.
Leather tongue would scream, if alive,
volcanic grit and acidic soil
cling like fire ants eating pink skin.

Mom smiles on command.

Dad's flaps his arms,
coaxes order from chaos.
With a click, click,
ghost-like images
etch black celluloid.

Before the camera clicks again,
Alan picks up his toy truck,
wonders out loud about our
artificial brick home on Lane Street,
now occupied now by strangers
from Arkansas.

When we left for camp,
Molly, Alan's dog, ran away,
disappeared like old paint
peeling in the wind
Mom holds Alan's hand,
licks her sleeve and wipes
a smudge from his face.

Minidoka fence gaps
reveal wide open spaces,
temptation for stir-crazy prisoners.

Desert so forbidding,
escape is certain death.
Wandering Twin Falls
in yellow skin, not an option.

Alan frowns at freedom beyond
barbed wire and declares,
"When I grow up,
I want to be white.
Being Japanese is too hard."

Brother Alan shoots a dead bead stare
at the guard tower while
German shepherds and tangled
barbed wire dance in the corners
of his eyes.

Stomach churns like horses
with tails afire,
when white soldiers
with bayonets and M-1 rifles
march past in step.

Mentally he erupts,
spews hot magma and ash,
burying thousands of inmates
frozen like statues.

Sleep offers no peace or salvation.
In rolling Hokusai waves,
reoccurring nightmares,
vertigo bed spins,
faceless monsters chase and claw,
hound him as his shoes
sink in quicksand.

Before jaws snap flesh,
a banshee's scream
pierces the barrack,
violates the silence again.

Mom Was Pregnant Over Half Her Time in Camp

Weaned on hard water,
mother's milk is laced with Spam,
macaroni and bitter rice.
Nutrition and weak bones
mom's daily fears for me.

Dirty diapers tortured until
stains and odors disappear,
back breaking wads scrubbed
across glass washboard ridges,
grating noises like a ride
on a bumpy road.

Mom's belly swells again,
creates a bumper car existence
of shoe horning into mess hall benches
and quick waddles to the gang latrine.

Army blanket walls
can't smother brother Alan's,
night terrors that
dart around the barracks
like rabid bats.

His cries overcome
sounds of coughs, and snores
beyond the blankets.

Born under the sign of Pisces,
two fish crossing paths,
I whimper as a baby.
Everyone is relieved,
not another screamer,
only a halting stammer
from a baldheaded baby.

Families whisper
about the whimpering
baby with no hair.

As an adult I write sad poems,
easy for someone who never
cried in Minidoka.

Poker night
in Block 33 Canteen,
worn cards shuffled
and dealt on thick olive-drab
army blanket.
Mandatory haze of blue
cigarette smoke hovers.

Dad squeezes his cards,
brags he's always lucky
when Mom is in the delivery room,
"Third time," he says.

He smiles a Cheshire grin
straight out of "Alice in Wonderland".

Dad raises and tosses all
his matchsticks in,
maybe a full boat to ride
or clever bluff.

Everyone folds. He jumps,
like a Vegas dice shooter,
gleefully shouts,
"Hubba hubba, come to Papa!

Baby needs new shoes."

Mr. Sato shuffles the cards, turns to Dad,
"Ernie, you brag about having kids and buying,
new shoes. Is that the best you can do when
your wife is killing herself every day in this prison?"

Return to Seattle from the Minidoka
Concentration Camp, 1945

Minidoka camp dies quickly.
Gone are: the mess halls,
forty-four barracks blocks, canteens
and guard towers. Prisoners with bus tickets
released like white doves in Idaho winds.

In Japan, our Hiroshima family home pancakes
on cousin Akio who nurses third degree burns
and scars from radioactive chaos.
Hiroshima is disorganized, confused.
No chance for us to live there.

We imitate salmon,
instinctively travel up stream
against the tide to Seattle—
settle in the Shirashi family basement
near Chinatown.

Cracked concrete walls,
three olive-drab army cots
are pushed into a corner.
Dresser drawer and folding chairs,
complete our home.

We celebrate Christmas
with mice, spiders and cobwebs.
Origami cranes made by Mom
dangle from a scrawny Christmas tree.
A flickering candle brightens the room.

Shell-shocked, we survive like moles
and fight the damp until we
grow stale like crackers.
Moldy in movements, we become
squatters infused with mildew,
odor embedded in our hair and clothes.

Upstairs Japanese New Years
Oshogatsu dinner: rice, seaweed,
sushi and Tai, fish bent and held

in position with toothpicks,
boiled shrimp, symbol of long life
"may you live until you bend over."
Celebration ensures a promising new year.

Mom dreams of returning to the Hiroshima,
family home 1,000 meters
from ground zero by the Motoyasu River
near the *Genbaku Dome.*

Brother Alan speaks only Japanese
when he attends kindergarten in Seattle.

One day at a time, like recovering
alcoholics, we lurch forward.

Fears and nightmares pursue us—
a second forced incarceration will come.

Quiet terror lurks like a drunk in the shadows,
steep cliffs of prejudice beckon
the next slip into icy crevasses below.

Lane Street Somnambulist 1950

Flying knees and elbows,
twirling dervish corkscrews
while asleep in bed.
Sheets and covers
twist my neck
like an umbilical cord.

My brother reports,
I sleepwalk to the front door,
turn the knob and jiggle
the handle to no avail.

Wind whips trees outside,
rain streams down window panes.
I hear nothing.

A savage lurks inside
who hunts like a wolf.
I wake exhausted with
no memory of the night.

Dr. Johnson recommends
a tonsillectomy to still
the Minidoka beast.

Orderlies help me down
a narrow waxed linoleum hallway
to a door with frosted glass.
I enter a cloud of thick medicinal odors,
see a nurse in white next to a small cot
behind vinyl curtains.

I wake and spit blood.
Vanilla ice cream
and Jello feed the beast—
wounded but still alive.

MY NAME IS YUTAKA

Mom always said, "Larry, your middle name, Yutaka,
means 'bamboo'. We named you after grandfather.
Bend but do not break."

Interviewing at the Boeing Company in the 1960s
I discover my official first name
is "Yutaka" as stated on my birth certificate,
not "Larry" as on my application form.

When Mother dies,
I vow to bend and not break.

Japanese friends correct my interpretation,
"Yutaka" means "Bounty not bamboo."

I find, I'm neither "Larry" or even bamboo.

Finally, I understand Mom's message:
wearing yellow skin in white America,
requires sleight of hand.

Sometimes small and sometimes big lies
are necessary to survive.

LEGACY

When hecklers circle a north Seattle
mosque after 9-11,
I won't turn my back
in silence knowing vultures
will descend on shuttered stores
and homes when hate
stains holy walls.

Who will stand
on granite mosque stairs,
link arms with brown brothers
and sisters?

I will stand for my
mother and father,
who sixty years ago
could not against US Army
bayonets, Browning rifles,
President Roosevelt
and Executive Order 9066.
I am like an alien abductee
who walks among
the living knowing the pain
and humiliation of being taken
while most white
Americans look away.

I have no nightmares about
gray creatures with spindly fingers
pushing needles into my belly button.

My stomach is a chunk of black basalt,
heavy like a meteorite, weight
that disappears only when I stand.

With only one lifetime to swing a pick,
toss dirt, haul ore, I hoist a lantern
in black tunnels, slide my hands
to atomic bonds, meld them
with stalactites and stalagmites of justice.

II.

MILK OF LIFE

Mother's milk, a hard water ooze.
Stones go walking under the moon.
Everything's gone except my bottle of booze.

My yellow skin, haters wish to bruise.
Unrealistic dreams of a better June;
mother's milk, a hard water ooze.

Holes pierce hand-me-down shoes.
Dust devils circle Minidoka dunes.
Everything's gone but my bottle of booze.

Texas Lost Battalion rescued, wonderful news.
Our liberation coming soon,
mother's milk, a hard water ooze.

Letters to Eleanor Roosevelt, nothing to lose
except metal meal trays or bent spoons.
Everything's gone except my bottle of booze.

We creep like cold molasses, my brain stews,
frustration rips like a tropical monsoon.
Mother's milk, it's a hard water ooze.
Everything gone but my bottle of booze.

Everyone in this photo is gone, except me.
Vitamin D deficiency and midnight crying,
square heads, floppy babies float on a dead sea.

Chilly weather kindles Mom's desire to be free,
Hiroshima nightmares visit after the bomb.
Everyone in this photo is gone, except me.

Uncle Bob resists becoming a draftee.
Block 44 boy drowns, rumors of a haunting.
Square heads, floppy babies float on a dead sea.

Skeletal deformities, soft skulls, and human debris,
like dirty diapers stack in the morning.
Everyone in this photo is gone, except me.

Malnutrition's shadows creep like ivy up a tree.
infants scream, in need of rocking.
Square heads, floppy babies float on a dead sea.

White nurses ignore rickets for me.
No sympathy for "Jap" children.
Everyone in this photo is gone, except me.
Square heads, floppy babies float on a dead sea.

Saturday Night Minidoka Swing Band Dance

A watercolor world of delicate gold and brown,
red and white streamers flutter and dance,
surreal leaves glow on the ground.

Saxophones blare as couples spin around.
Swirling faces, I shoot a seductive glance,
in a watercolor world of delicate gold and brown.

She is a Durer angel with roses her crown.
Her lithe body glides a swan's death dance.
Surreal leaves glow on the ground.

We float on mess hall floors without a sound,
eyes-lock, leave nothing to chance,
in this watercolor world of delicate gold and brown.

Idaho full moon shimmers on her tea-dyed gown.
Minidoka Swing Band blares a hypnotic trance.
Surreal leaves glow on the ground.

We are ancient mummers with spirits bound.
Under guard towers we yearn for romance.
In a watercolor world of delicate gold and brown
surreal leaves glow on the ground.

Dervish of flying knees and elbows.
Her water breaks before the new moon.
Fruit flies sparkle in morning sunlight.

Fat robins squawk like hungry crows,
slumbering larva torn from a silky cocoon.
Dervish of flying knees and elbows.

Mother dreams of Mt. Rainier snow.
Hopes baby delivery comes soon.
Fruit flies sparkle in blazing sunlight.

Hand-me-downs for baby clothes.
Mom swelters all afternoon,
Dervish of flying knees and elbows.

Stork backlog, deliveries run slow.
Bottom smacked, to screams, and swoons.
Fruit flies sparkle in blazing sun.

Slant eyes foreshadow future woes.
Melancholic dirges among favorite tunes.
Dervish of flying knees and elbows.
Fruit flies sparkle in blazing sunlight.

III.

Anthem to the White Lady Who Runs a Japanese Antique Shop

In a Sandra Bullock film, this quaint town was a New England
    village.
Her candle shop was across the street near the boardwalk
    overlooking the bay.

I stroll past the pizza restaurant and inhale the crisp sea air.
"This is what it feels like to walk freely
like a human being without a care."

I glance up at a Japanese antique shop sign. The brass bell
on the door continues to ring after I enter.

The owner, an older white lady greets me like a friend.
She asks, "And where were you born?" I smile and wonder
how she could begin a sentence with "And" as if this was
an on-going conversation.

The customers sense the unfolding drama,
lean forward in anticipation.

"I know this scenario," I muse. This is her opportunity to extoll
the virtues of my culture and gush about her time in Japan
and praise the industry of my so very nice people.

I pause, play dumb, then turn to my audience.
With gusto I announce,
"I was born in Idaho is that in the USA?"
Before she can backtrack and say she meant my parents
or kin and not me, I slather the frosting on my remark and plop
    the cherry on top.

"It was a concentration camp in Idaho, is that in America?
And where were you born?"

Big Box Hardware Store During the Pandemic

Circles embedded in the floor
with footprint decals
mark six feet distances
for customers to observe.
I move from decal to decal.

Behind carts loaded with lumber and
baskets of merchandise, I reach
the register and request my "Veteran's" discount.

Only my eyes are visible
under my camo Seahawks cap
and white N-95 mask,

I lift one gallon of white paint
for a ride on the conveyor belt.
Give my phone number.

Shielded by Plexiglas,
the masked cashier
examines me and asks:

"What military?"

"This is a new one," I think.
"Maybe I should say 'Chinese Communist',
French Foreign Legion, or British Grenadiers."

Instead, I squint my eyes tight
like surgical slits and reply,
"I'm in your computer, check it."

Under flying Gothic arches
of Suzzallo Library,
amid leather-bound books
and stained-glass windows,
Gordon drops a heap and clatter
of samurai armor.

Protection forged from:
Giri (duty), *Gaman* (perseverance)
and *Shikata ga nai* (it can't be helped).
During meditations,
bolt-like visions of purity strike
a contemplative Gordon, cleanses
his soul under

an invigorating rapture
of cascading pacifism.
Quaker shields of love
and harmony embrace.

Glistening soldier of peace awakes,
unfolds like a lotus from curfew's
mud-filled darkness.
Armed with truth, he hoists
a red lantern buffeted by devil winds
and blasts of injustice.
America must fulfill its promise.

So that innocents are never taken again
and a healing balm soothes Japanese
American grief, holy grail of justice
becomes his quest.

As a symbol of principled determination,
Gordon is a lightning bolt
of calmness piercing blackness
that shrouds the Golden Gate,
the wheat fields of Kansas,
and Lady Liberty's torch.

Mom's smile hides
her *soppa* embarrassment,
slight protrusion of
upper front incisors,
buck teeth, some would say
with a snicker.

Soppa, her self-conscious shame,
blemish her hand habitually covers
when she speaks and smiles,
gesture mistaken for shyness
that distinguishes her
from look-alike
Minidoka women.

Inside the fence she is a proud mother,
grips Alan's hand tight
and slogs muddy paths between
tar paper barracks.

Behind barbed wire, no fears of racist barbs,
or easy-speak "Viola" name,
scorched like a cattle brand
by white Franklin High
school teachers who refused
to call her "Hanae".

They Called Her "Viola"

"Hanae, such a pretty Japanese name,
but a bit difficult," remarked Miss Sanders
the 10th grade English teacher.

"Class from now on we will call her Viola,
a musical flourish like a show tune
in a Broadway play,
variation of Violet,
fragrant flower."

Name change rubs Hanae
like iron chains and handcuffs.

Miss Sanders quotes Shakespeare,
after the transformation,
"A rose is a rose."

Hanae's Franklin High School
1934 annual brims with entries,
"Viola, fun knowing you.
Viola, good luck in the future."

After June graduation speeches,
dignitaries file from the stage.
Hanae flips her tassel,
clutches the mortar board,
launches it midair.
Ecstatically discards "Viola"
like a worn out sock.

She becomes a J-town girl again,
embraces her Hiroshima roots,
recalls tranquil waters of the Motoyasu River
flowing by the family home
and wonders what the future holds.

SILK PURSE FROM A SOW'S EAR

For 1942 Japanese American Residents of the
Minidoka, Idaho Concentration Camp

Mothball fragrances billow
from our clothes.
We resemble deserts.
Coarse like corn cobs,
hard tack, and artisan bread crust,

parched lips, cracked and prickly
barbed wire hands, snagged
tumbleweed spirits, sticky hair,
gnarly sagebrush bodies.

Our camp apartment:
dressers scavenged from wood scrap heaps,
dangling naked light bulbs,
black and white striped
mattress ticking stuffed
with straw, olive-drab army
blankets curtains droop,
sentinels of privacy.

As outcasts and packrats,
being proper Americans
and human beings
is a shadow memory.
Instead we float like
washed up by Idaho's
hard water: liquid concoction
of calcium and magnesium
that dries and brittles.

Six-year old Alan stares and squints
at wooden machine gun towers,
expression stolen from white guards.

Mom brushes dirt from his canvas pants,
daubs my baby blanket
in her saliva and wipes away
breakfast stains from his cheek.

Proud in itchy sweaters,
yarn ripped from old shawls,
we wear lumpy wool woven
like scratchy burlap potato sacks.

Shirts with elbow patches
and mismatched oversized buttons
complement shoes past their time
lined with Twin Falls newspaper insoles.

Mom wears a maroon sweater,
a shade beyond purple
with a heavy dose of red,
eye catching in an unnatural way.

We board the bus to town
on a medical day pass.
White mothers and children
stroll Twin Falls sidewalks.

Without a word or missed step,
paths open for us,
like Moses parting the Red Sea,

Not respect or courtesy,
but fear of medieval maladies
and unnatural calamities
that might befall them
if drilled by our slant eyes.

Block 26 Reunion Picnic, 1952

Crowds make Dad nervous.
Social interaction fears
eat his stomach lining.
In perpetual mental frenzy,
he sits at home alone.

At the Block 26 reunion picnic,
Mom resembles a carefree
teenager in bobby socks
and two-tone saddle shoes.

She raises her arms
in victory after crossing
the gunny sack race finish line.

Her Minidoka poisons under control,
virulent contagion held
beneath a thin veneer
that breaks occasionally,
and sends black rain,
to fall on us, her children.

A torrent, we don't understand
or able to handle, makes us
want to scream.

Mom almost spits when speaking
about goiters and skin boils,
she explains how prejudice
put us in camps.

Too young to know,
we visualize "prejudice"
as a train rolling down a track.

She says, "Pneumonia sent Cousin Johnny
to Tacoma General from Camp Harmony.
When he heard the head nurse said,
'Just let the Jap kid die.'
He screamed that he wanted to go home."

White people remember
Pearl Harbor after the war.
Our parents drill us daily,
everything we do reflects
on the community.

Bachi ga attaru, the universe will strike
if you do something wrong.
Bachi ga attata, something bad happens
because of an earlier misdeed.
We behave and do well in school,
afraid of shaming the community.

News reports a Japanese teen
lost for days mushroom hunting.
We worry about trouble he causes
white people and attention he draws.
KING TV shows a rescue team
proudly carrying him from the forest.
The boy raises his arms in victory
celebrating as if a hero.
I am amazed they searched
inspite of the fact he was Japanese.

Community gossip spreads
about the boy's dishonorable behavior,
black eye he caused.
"Something must be mentally
wrong with him."

POWER OF LIES

When "But" appears in a sentence, it means
everything before it is not necessarily true.

With hand over heart,
as a six-year old,
I recite the Pledge of Allegiance,

"Liberty and Justice for All."

"But" inserts itself years later:

George Floyd
Gordon Hirabayashi
Trail of Tears
Breonna Taylor
Trevon Martin
Miscegenation laws
Black Lives Matter
Fred Korematsu
Voter suppression
Anti-Chinese riots
Charleena Lyles
Zoot suit riots
Anti-Asian Hate
Segregation
Voter suppression
Anti-abortion laws
Roe V. Wade Overturned

Is "Liberty and Justice for All"
nothing more than:
fake news, conspiracy theories,
and alternative facts or is it
a promise America intends to keep?

Walking down the street
with no fears of being pushed in front
of subway trains or smacked with a
bag of rocks, would be a start.

The Fallen

Nisei fall down seven times, rise up again.
In Rainier's shadow, sacred torii beckons like Mt. Fuji,
welcome sight after our release from WWII desert prisons.
Cherry blossoms flutter a blanket of pink snow.

IV.

Enola Gay and the Big Bomb

Leaded glass fractures sunlight, bursts
into seven tinctured bands.

A son should not precede his father into night.

Prismatic faces explode and invite
vibrations that transmute a Handel overture.
Leaded glass fractures sunlight.

Retina's lining magnetizes energy, rods excite
holographic images replicated in miniature.

A son should not precede his father into night.

Heat, flash, radiation brightness
crystallizes two eyes in rapture.
Leaded glass fractures sunlight.

An atom bomb explodes: molecules ignite—
physical bodies sundered beyond cure.
Leaded glass fractures sunlight.

A son should not precede his father into night.

TASTE OF BETRAYAL—CHRISTMAS AT LANE STREET, 1949

Flames leap, kiss the glass stove portal,
convex transparent cover tames
raging orange and blue flames,
hell's broth Santa could never navigate.

Mom unwraps and sorts gifts
warmed by orange flames.
Best gifts go to Hiroshima relatives,
nuclear holocaust survivors.

Leftovers belong to us.
Mom winks as she pushes
a present across the yellow
linoleum floor towards us.

Like a game of Red Rover
a black fruitcake container adorned
with two pink orchids comes over.

We leap with excitement.
Circular wonder of overflowing promise,
volcanic mass held hostage under
a film of red cellophane.

It's a gooey lump laden with candied citron,
orange peels and maraschino cherries
embedded in a thick dark clump.

I ready my mouth to receive this goodness,
bite the sticky mass sprinkled with
fragments of sweetness.

I growl, immediately resent my cousin's
begging, their atomic bomb excuses,
and Mom's willingness
to favor them above us.

My Reoccurring Childhood Nightmares:

Mushroom clouds loom.
Elliott Bay boils as
Russian bombers nuke Seattle
on a sunny afternoon.
White men in black suits
and fedoras chase me.
It begins when the world is quiet
then moves faster and faster
like a merry-go-round
twirling out of control,
ripping hinges
from the door.

At night I toss sheets.
Mom stacks pillows
to soften my frequent
falls to the floor.

I fight sleep, ponder possible nuclear
devastation. Visualize a desert
wasteland scattered with Hiroshima skeletons.

My foot dangles like an anchor,
bumps bottom but never grabs hold,
weak attempt to stop my spinning world.

Hiroshima Family Grave-1995

Gray granite monument
with black Japanese script,
our family grave holds
a small drawer of ashes.
Nearby hundreds of upright markers
squeeze like a stone garden into a cemetery
bound by apartment buildings
inside the middle of the city.

Cousin Akira slides the drawer open,
maybe 1,000 years of ancestors
layered like sediment on the ocean floor.
Mentally I drill a core sample down
to the first Yamadas,
origins of my mother's family tree.
My hands want to reach into
samurai, merchants, housewives,
bomb victims and civil servants.

Maybe only 50 years of ancestors there
if the bomb converted ashes to ashes,
spread remains to the wind,
dust on the "tansu", grime and pollution
precipitated from the air.

Rain falls into the granite box,
pock-marking the ashes.
The sound of rain on ashes,
blunted music from the sky.

I touch the stone, remember Minidoka
and my own Seattle grave under a red maple
in the Japanese section of Washelli's Cemetery
—American ghetto to ghetto.

Five cousins in blue surround me,
hold black umbrellas.
One who looks like mother,
shelters and protects me.
I gaze into my ancestors' remains.
Exhale a cleansing breath.

In this small drawer of ashes, my thoughts
return to incarnations where I'm free
to roam as *Ronin*, master-less samurai,
centuries before Minidoka poisons
flow in my veins.

V.

Cleveland H.S. Study Hall, 1963

I doodle cartoons,
squares, and triangles,
clock hands don't move.

When most girls desire
Sandra Dee looks,
a Marilyn imitator
sits in front of me.
She scribbles hearts
and "Marilyn Monroe"
over her yellow Pee Chee.

"You should be in gym,"
I mumble.

To my surprise she replies,
"Marilyn Monroe had holes
in her undies, never
suited up for gym."

"That's not true," I say.
She winks.

Curious, I never noticed her before.
I ask, "soda tonight?"
She shakes her head,
says, "No, don't want anyone
to see where I live."

"Marilyn," I reply,
"how about I close my eyes?"

She looks like a bag of potatoes
in her boucle sweater,
Marilyn and I stroll
Laguna unnoticed.
Playfully she bumps me.
Dimples sparkle
when the ocean breeze
catches her hair.

"Bet you a quarter you
can't do the Marilyn,"
I challenge.

She tucks her sweater,
pouts her red lips,
hums "I wanna be loved,
boopie boppie do."

Her lungs swell
and hot cross buns
balloon in petal-pushers.
Sidewalks shrink
with the ba bump,
ba bump, ba bump,
of Marilyn's heart.

Wolf whistles and catcalls
spill from construction crews.
Marilyn's sloe-eyed
smile quiets the beasts,
lambs bleat when she
cradles my hand,
kisses my cheek.

Marilyn the Goddess, Shape-Shifter

Short and chunky,
she dons a tattered
terry cloth robe and wraps
a towel turban above her
cold cream smeared face.

In an hour she is thinner
with longer legs,
a goddess whose skin
photographs like living flesh.
The legend *motates* down Park Avenue,
New York cabby necks crane,
parked trucks smash.

Mobs clamor and shove.
They lust with expectations
of immediate gratification—
hunger for a taste of this
ice cream sundae
atop a fuming volcano.
Dumb blond bombshell persona,
her ticket to stardom,
binds the same way
my skin holds me captive.
Strangers are my mirror.

Marilyn reveals her secrets,
how I can transform from
Japanese houseboy looks
and shape-shift into a king.
Become a loose hipped Elvis
gyrating in nothing but
a jock strap and blue suede shoes.

ACTOR'S STUDIO

Her actor's studio outfit—teddy bear coat,
white bobby socks, saddle shoes,
blonde hair tucked under a black scarf.

She is like a kitten with sunglasses
curling in a corner
comfort-nest-purring—

> copy of "Ulysses", dog eared
> where they kiss
> under the Moorish wall
> and his heart
> beats like mad.

White leather satchel purse—

> Silver Coney Island
> Good Luck-Good Luck
> horseshoe key ring charm
> with a penny in the center.

> Black Sheaffer fountain pen and envelop
> with a poem fragment scrawled,
> what we might think about if
> we think about l'amour.

> Black and white photo
> of Maf, her white poodle
> from Sinatra.

Gold tube of Revlon Fatal Apple lipstick.

Prescription plastic pharmacy tube—

> White cotton stuffing,
> pink pills, Nembutal,
> something to bring sleep.

BLONDE DE BLONDE

"Joltin' Joe" DiMaggio
peers at Times Square
on a hot New York evening.
Movie lights cascade over
Marilyn fighting her rising skirt
above a subway grate,
enjoying each gust.

She is Brut Champagne
from a fire hose nozzle,
California Blonde de Blonde,
cork popper, sassy, nose tickler.

Cops on horseback
corral frenzied fans who
scream for another
burst of effervescence.

She gushes magic
that men steal home
in brown paper bags,
hide under mattresses
away from the wife and kids.

Not Marilyn's first or last
"back alley" visit.
Studios don't groom
pregnant starlets.

The cold exam table
and stirrups are bookend
mates to the casting couch.

All the show girls
know the little man
in a dingy office over
a funeral parlor
who is one step above
a bent coat hanger jockey.

He gives no eye contact,
fidgets and drags
on a "Lucky" he leaves
in the ashtray next to her,
it burns to a stub.

Sweat beads
on his forehead
and thin upper lip.
Red neon lights
reflect in his eyeglasses.

A pale Marilyn
shivers in silence
on shards of glass.
She glows white
under the glare
of a naked light bulb.

MADISON SQUARE GARDEN BIRTHDAY PARTY

"Thank you I can now retire from politics after
having had ...ah "Happy Birthday" sung to me in
such a sweet, wholesome way."
President Kennedy, May 19th 1961

Tight on champagne
she writhes in a dress
that Houdini could not escape.
Peter Lawford introduces
the "late" Marilyn Monroe.

She sings a breathy
"Happy Birthday" to JFK
who chomps hard on his cigar.
Flash bulbs pop white hot,
shrink and crinkle brown.

In a black tux, Kennedy
commands the spotlight.
Marilyn stands in darkness,
most glamorous woman
in the world, alone again.

She pulls on a black wig.
Dark glasses cover tears
on the way to LaGuardia Airport.

Marilyn plays her final game
of seduction, submission, and rejection,
Russian Roulette with sleeping pills.
She pulls the trigger amid rumors
her hospital visit scraped away
a piece of Camelot.

Sex Goddess Accompanies Arthur Miller-June 1956
House Committee on Un-American Activities Testimony

I recall 60 years ago
when House representatives,
snacked on dismembered writers
like hungry lions.

Under the spotlight's glare,
Arthur avoids shade
or skirts to duck behind.

Marilyn does the "Bump de Bump",
kidnaps center stage,
her bulging curves
scream for liberation,
like 100 pounds of potatoes
in a 50-pound sack.

Flash bulbs burst.
Her image freezes,
atom bomb silhouettes
burned into white walls.

Marilyn blinks away camera blue dots.
She wiggles and tugs
her hiked up skirt.

VaVa Voom!

Arthur imitates John Wayne
and shouts, "I'll take this bridge alone."

Emerging from a smoldering crucible,
he sheds his translucent skin and brags.
"That'll teach them who's boss."

Today, under the same House lights,
Trump would whine, "Witch hunt."

Marilyn Monroe Hammock Blues

Marilyn snuggles deep
in a cocoon tethered to date palms.
I sneak up behind her.

She drops "Ulysses" on the rattan table,
adjusts her sunglasses
and warns, "Don't you dare."

Marilyn recounts her movie studio visit:

> Louie has this *Glacier* script.
> 'Don't take my darling boy away.'
> is my big line.

> Practiced it a thousand times—soft, hard,
> slow and with a southern drawl.
> Fat bald Louie opens the door
> and shouts, 'America loves you!'

> The *Glacier* is his excuse to be
> a riptide and tear my bodice open.
> Afterwards I feel like pigeon poop.

> Instead of gagging, I smile.
> Turn stage right and deliver my line,
> 'Don't take my darling boy away.'

> Who says I can't act?

She pauses and searches between hard covers,
flips to the last page of "Ulysses".

Tired of being Marilyn,
she asks to be alone.

Just a Short Note to Say Something You Already Know

for Ivanka Trump

Ivanka, in a different time and place,
you and your children are squeezed into
cattle cars destined for Nazi death camps.
Stars pinned to your coats
and numbers tattooed on your arms.
Religion is your crime, a variation
on other exclusions like the 120,000
Japanese Americans whose race
incarcerates them during World War II.

If you dodge head shaving,
and starvation, maybe a country
would welcome you.

Angel of Death is difficult to slip,
unfortunates are turned away,
chased by verbal brickbats and pitchforks.
You smell freedom's scent
but only glimpse porthole view
of Lady Liberty's tantalizing torch.

Doors slam and hands
of kindness withdraw.
You are not among privileged
huddled masses.

Today as a 1% American demographic,
you are safe by an accident of birth.
Others less fortunate, however,
stand on precipices knowing,
"History does not repeat
itself, but it rhymes."

When Donald promises
a magnificent Great Wall
and spews religious
hatred to cheering crowds,
you must feel a guilty twinge
realizing if this were 1943 Germany,

a chorus of incendiary voices
would echo and push innocents, including you
off slippery cliffs into eternal darkness.

Black hole so forbidding victims
never see their children again
as the self-serving politicians parade
on bandwagons swerving on and off
a broken ashen highway, and the shards
of bones from the eight million dead
grind under their wheels.

Unlike the Walrus and Carpenter

We enter the poem on slippery rocks
and ruffled oyster shells.
Torches serpentine through darkness,
shucking knives click as oysters pop,
rows of meaty half shells glow like
the Cantina scene from Star Wars.
Amid swirling low-tide perfumes
and crashing surf music,
crackling wood embers tango and spiral
like fireflies in the wind.

We are night marchers in rubber boots,
slick raingear, and piercing spelunker headlights.
Instinctively we migrate as if magnetized
by shucking bars teeming with Kumamotos, Shigokus
and Olympias. Head beams crisscross
like prison search lights and disappear
among wine bars, shuckers, and darkness
enveloping the beach.

We lose ourselves in oyster moments.
Discover enlightenment in briny flavors of gills
and glycogen chewed slowly as if full of pearls
until we savor plankton, somewhere down
the food chain. Cold Pinot Grigo cleanses the palate.

Like zealots we slurp and casually toss
dead soldiers with a flick of the wrist.
This tale has no trolls, wicked queens,
or unhappy endings. Fearless, we live
in the moment's cacophony
and revel with newfound friends.

Experiencing old world magical
phantasms that connect us to all living creatures
seems like a dream in the morning.
But my body remembers buttery morsels fit for the gods
that launch us like Roman candles. Wine glasses explode,
oyster shooters fly, and the law of gravity is repealed.
Unfettered and no longer 'down to earth',
we levitate freely, tango madly with the stars.

La Medusa Cooking Class

for Chef Julie

If I am Semolina,
Jules scoops handfuls of me,
chops spinach and mixes parsley.
Egg yolks cement a green lump.

With loving thumps and tender spanks,
she wraps me tight in Saran.
I burst when her red lips
caress my body. Wooden rolling pins
and wine bottles whirl.

With a crank of the pasta machine
she squeezes me flat,
presses me to her cheeks,
and drapes me over wooden dowels.
I am stretched—green chalk-ugly,
flaccid and grainy.

Jules teases green bowties,
curls angel hairs and fettuccine ribbons.
She spares napalm garlic
and dresses me with simmering duck legs,
aubergine figs, fresh peas, cracked olives,
topped with pea vines.

One mouthful of green
and she is my pasta slave.

VI.

What's on My Desk

Something for a wish—

carved wooden bear

brown paws folded in his lap,

salmon in his belly.

Photo-shopped Marilyn

Monroe flapper magnet,

embroidered lace,

feather headband,

eyes cast down.

Slider sinker rig,

fishing line swivel

and rusty clip.

Two red *darumas* without eyes,

weights in the bottom,

six times on the ground

seven times upright.

ALLISON THE FRAMER

"I only have eyes for you".
The Flamingos, on the oldies station

Allison rushes from the beauty salon,
to her art frame shop on the "Ave".
She sports newly minted blonde streaks
and a tight perm.

Gazing out the bus window,
she imagines frames around everything
including the tree on the corner
accompanied by a green mat to bring out the leaves.

Allison jumps off and rushes into the Allegro
for a quick lunch,
settles at a funky table
and orders a ham and cheese.

From the corner of her eye
she catches a woman staring.

"Annoying but something familiar about her," she thinks.
The woman frowns and squints.

Allison wonders:

> Is she a customer?
> An old friend?
> Nice looking.
> Maybe she is gay.
> Or maybe my birth mother?

Allison bites her lip and walks towards her.

A thick black frame

holds a mirror and reflects a face
that sports a tight perm and streaks.

Allison gasps and laughs.

Back home, Tangie, the cockatoo,
loves Allison's parakeet, Pete.
But Pete cares only for
that handsome green bird
in the mirror next to the feeder.
No room in his heart for Tangie.

POSTCARD FROM MEXICO

The San Blas surf disappeared as I buried
her last postcard in the garden.
Twelve sunflowers sprouted, grew ripe
bending like old men.

I imagined the breeze swelling from the Pacific
and saw her writing at Miguel's café.
She licked the salt off the margarita glass and wrote,
"Think of me when you plant sunflowers."

BULLETS

When I turn 75 in March,
Charlie and I will dig up the five-gallon plastic box
of ammo I buried in the garden for the apocalypse.
We'll unpack the 22 and 30-30 shells.
Drive to the mud bank in back of his Enumclaw barn,
and shoot cans like we did in the Arizona desert.

I remember the spring of 1976
when we proudly packed our pistols,
hiked through the Superstitions,
looking for outlaw camps and rattlesnakes.
All we ever saw were cactus and other hikers
with bigger guns than ours.

SEEING YOUR MOTHER'S BIRTHDAY MEMORIAL PHOTOS ON FACEBOOK

For Erin, in honor of Deborah

I grieve for truth lost,
like you for your mother
on her day and every day.

Memories rise like the autumn wind.
I shuffle over a leaf strewn
   street in slow motion near
   Queen Anne Avenue North.

   Recalling my mother's touch,
   I'm transformed into a six-year old
   peddling my red tricycle.

Wheel spokes spin prayers to heaven,
   release a bolt from outer space,
   careening image meant for you:

Deborah dances under the Big Dipper,
waltz she couldn't perform
after being prematurely stricken.
She glows translucent, smiles,
reaches for your outstretched hand.

VII.

KETA, COUSINS OF KING SALMON

Twenty feet from home,
leaping Keta salmon
ram craters into locked
hatchery chain-linked gates.

Splashes and thuds
echo through the Alaskan night.
There is no weak link.

Trains of relentless
missiles thud
lasting impressions
in the fence.

Keta eggs waste,
swirl, and spill
aimlessly downstream.

The gene pool ends
for those outside the fence.
Fingerlings feed on what drifts by,
grow strong and head to sea.

I Do Not Believe in Hell

As an eight-year old,
we discuss the merciful God
concept in Presbyterian Sunday school.
I realize my best friends are Buddhist.

"What happens to good people
who do not believe?" I ask.

Like a television revival minister,
my Sunday school teacher looks me in the eye,
shakes his finger and declares, "non-believers
will burn in hell."

I visualize the Buddhist Cub
Scout Troop 242 marching
the winding road to Hades
while the young Lotus Skyliner
dance band strikes up a hot tune.

"How do I break the news to them?"

Fifty years later my friend, Tets,
whose father, grandfather, great grandfather
and great-great grandfather were Buddhist priests,
answers my Sunday school question.

"We are not going to hell," he declares,
"because we don't believe in it."

It is a striking revelation
like Newton's apple falling—
"we shall go wherever we believe,"
I conclude.

When Dad is on his
Kamada Nursing home deathbed,
Mom calls Pastor Tanaka
to baptize Dad as a Christian,
stealing his soul from grasps of
his Buddhist mother and 1,000 ancestors.

No holy water sprinkled,
Reverend kneels and prays,
not enough juice to propel Dad
through the pearly gates.

Dad passes believing in nothing,
heaven's door slammed and dead-bolted shut,
abandons Mom to be in Christian heaven,
angry as hell.

MINIDOKA MISCARRIAGE

They took us to camp and we didn't want to go.
When the war ended, kicked us out, even though
we had nowhere to go.
Hanae Matsuda

Fetus discarded like hazardous
waste, partial jawbone in a lumpy mass,
flesh that bypasses the Minidoka cemetery,
where 400 rest.

Buddhist urns and Christians' coffins,
three to six feet deep,
headstones line the gritty soil
near a basalt fence.

Some Nisei KIAs remain
in France, others rest
in Arlington and Minidoka.
What of Issei who committed suicide
immediately before their release?
No relatives or homes, twenty-five dollars
and a train ticket would have been their farewell.

Minidoka gates fall open, electricity
shuts and barbed wire cut. Headstones are
bulldozed and stacked in heaps
resemble bones in the catacombs.
Like dew they evaporate quickly
taken by who knows who
to who knows where.

Officially, all dead exhumed
like archeological treasures
and sent home if possible.

Barracks sawed in half
and hauled away by lucky land
lottery winners. White homesteaders claim
Minidoka piece by piece.

Cemetery transformed into blankets of golden
barley as on Murphy's nearby farm.
Some recall grave markers somewhere,
others whisper about remains.

Sixty-seven years later, a headstone
with *kanji* emerges from
a swimming hole like a raised fist.

Large stones go walking
like night marchers
under the Idaho full moon,
seek cool waters of the Snake.

Ghosts stir as John Deere
tractors plow and mix horse manure
into fields that once held 400 Japanese graves.

In historic black and white photos
families pose by headstones.
Their faces stark and hollow.

Over the years, graveyard stories fade
and blink away, lost footnotes.

Uncle Arnie, the Sanitarian

"Sanitarian", term Uncle Arnie
gives his hands compulsive
and incessant scrubbing.

How did Arnie survive Minidoka? I wonder.
Imagined him shuffling through barracks
in a full body suit like a Black
Plague medieval doctor
with a bird beak mask stuffed
full of protective herbs:
black brimmed witch hat, a cane
to touch contaminated things
and gloves to lift door latches.

How did the germ phobic Arnie
survive gang latrine stench,
stained metal trough urinals,
and outhouse style commodes
complete with green flies circling?

What of mess hall utensils
cemented with white rice
and germ bombs expelled
by neighbors behind army
blanket curtain walls?

What of dust that rises
from floors like airborne gnats
and settles as scum
on his Buddhist shrine?

Dust sparkles luminous floaters,
like fruit flies shining
in shafts of sunlight.

After camp we visit Arnie in his
public housing apartment in Seattle.
Wary of friendly fire, he writhes
slowly with a facial grimace
as he feigns civility and courtesy
knowing we are laden
with infectious microbes.

He sits at the kitchen table
like an abandoned dog
burdened with nameless guilt and fear.

He buttons a blue cardigan sweater,
dons a white scarf like a mask,
hollow eyes resemble
a deathbed patient.

Arnie avoids eye contact,
believes stares transmit disease
in a teeming world of organisms that feed
like hook worms burrowing into his body.

Yet he rises every morning
to sip green tea knowing each day
will bring terror.

Patiently he waits for evening
for his friend, darkness, to slip under his door.

Uncle Arnie's Funeral, 1956

Alabaster visage rests in satin underbrush.
Embalming fluids in worn-out veins,
casket wheels roll waves beneath the crush.

Bronze temple bell ring fades to a blush,
grandchildren fold 1,000 origami cranes.
Alabaster visage emerges from satin underbrush.

Anti-germicidal sprays no longer a rush.
Mourners' line snakes like an old steam train.
Casket wheels push waves beneath the crush.

Arnie's white porter gloves, invisible at first blush.
Five magnificent wreaths demand a hush.
Like sentinals they stand near floral chains.
Alabaster visage rests in satin underbrush.

Germicidal sprays no longer a rush.
Yellow ribbons flutter in the rain.
Casket wheels push waves beneath the crush.

He abhored Minidoka filth and sagebrush,
dreamt of drinking French champagnes.
Alabaster visage emerges from satin underbrush.
Casket wheels roll waves beneath the crush.

Cracked mosaic design scars hospital floors.
Faded green and brown patterns glide like wax
under my mother's locked door.

Imagined colored tiles cradling Skagit's
spawning Chinooks. Fingerlings, like dots
and dashes, escape from orange cages,
feast on nutrient rich carcasses disintegrating in shallows.

Each mouthful carries prehistoric memories of:

    chasing hordes of silver herring,
    ravaging clouds of floating krill,
    and tasting fluttering ribbons
    of the Skagit River 3,000 miles from home.

Unable to touch mother or my ancestor's ashes
deep in Hiroshima boxes, spirits
guide me like a minnow to the Salish Sea.

Skagit River bonfires crisscross rocky shores.
Their smoldering signal beacons call me home.

I stand alone, barefooted and crooked, shard
of grey in a stream of fractured tiles.

    I peer through wire-meshed glass
into mother's empty room,
recall her over-the- glasses smile.

Seattle Covid-19 Pandemic Brain Damage: 2020-2021

For Mayor Durkan and the Seattle City Council

Like the chained prisoner in Plato's
allegory of the cave, reality becomes
shadows—dancing television images.

I see downtown tent multiplexes
squeezed on pedestrian sidewalks,
bags of human litter frozen midstream,
glacial flow sliding downhill.

Concrete chunks crash like meteorites
hurled on to Interstate 90—
commuters hug the left lanes for safety
as police watch helplessly.
Mentally incompetent perps. are released,
do not stand trial in a sordid
game of "Whack a Mole"
where offenders return freely to their nests.

Chinatown and Japantown resemble New Orleans
after a hurricane—
windows boarded, graffiti spreads
like kudzu to freeway
exit signs and nearby buildings,

Capitol Hill grocery clerk helplessly begs
a masked man to stop stuffing his
backpack and pay for groceries.

Red and green rental bikes
are strewn as if thrown by a giant,
tripping hazards for the blind and elderly.

On Market Street in Ballard, I saw
a green bike suspended on a telephone
pole ten feet in the air while others
were thrown into Lake Union.

Dorothy and Toto would drop their jaws,
realizing it isn't 2018 anymore.

At 3:00 AM outside my house,
metal sawing wakes me,
a black Toyota truck with no
license plates slips into darkness,
carries a load of catalytic converters.

In my residential neighborhood,
a Parking Enforcement
officer tickets parked cars
that encroach on sidewalks.
He explains that walkways must
be accessible for wheelchairs
and people on crutches.

On Thursdays I make
my weekly provision run to Costco.
Though fully vaccinated,
I mask up and consciously behave
like I've received no shots,
first mental step to avoid
a visit from Mr. Death.

I treat everyone like lepers,
maintain social distance, and carry a cane
for self-defense, a stick to ward off
Asian haters twirling plastic
bags full of rocks aimed at my head.

Outside I scan the streets
and parking lots like a sniper,
walk in fear I might harm
someone who attacks me.
Being mentally competent,
defending myself means risking
hard time for assault and battery.

BRUSH WITH DEATH

Northwest Salmon spirits
in red and black tribal robes guide me
to a secret fishing place.

Green waters cradle Skagit's
spawning Chinooks.

Transparent fishing line
hisses mid-air and splay akimbo.
I slip but right myself immediately,
worry my hip boots would fill
and take me down river.
Quickly I drop my boots on shore.

I stand alone, barefooted and crooked
like a grey stone in a stream of flowing green.
My mission—to kill salmon.

In black waders and grey duster,
Mr. Death sidles up to me,
casts his line over mine.

I retrieve a twisted wad,
something that water creatures
knitted together.

I examine a cat's cradle of snags
and feel his cold breath on my neck.
He rasps, "Nothing to worry about.
Just a routine visit, my friend."

Detour

Don't weep for me

At night I search internet afterlife sites,
But cable television re-runs
steal my attention, divert me
with episodes of: Bigfoot plaster casts,
Da Vinci Code, UFOs sightings, crop circles,
Civil War ghosts, mermaids attacking
sea monsters and Atlantis sinking.

Back on task, I learn just before death,
Christian lives flash before them
engulfed by white light.
Tunnels open to a quiet place
where thoughts instantly
become reality: gamblers win,
miners hit glory holes,
and parties go on forever,
until spirits tire of earthly things.
Christian souls ride
the after-life conveyor belt
to God's throne.

No flash backs for young children.
Instead imaginary futures leap forward:
adolescence, adulthood, marriage,
children, old age, death and a trip
to Jesus's throne.

Merciful God gives all the full ride, regardless.

Buddhist souls recycle like empty
plastic containers and bypass
white light.

Agnostic believers burst like
dismembered atoms, transform into
cosmic scatter-shots of energy
sprinkled through eternity that
dance like stars in the heavens.

Before stepping into God's light,
I will snag a detour in my green boat,
troll Salmon grounds in mystical seas.

My dog, Cookie, and I will chase wild Chinook
beyond the Milky Way through
timeless rivers and quiet inlets,
past spiritual kelp beds around
gentle corners of eternity.

My Father Who Art Not in Heaven

At the Washelli cemetery
Mom and Dad rest side by side
like eggs in a carton,
separated by concrete
but most of all religion.

Father, an atheist, dies to wander in space
or reincarnates like a television re-run.
Mom and brother Alan
await my arrival in Christian heaven.

I ponder, "How can Mom and Dad reunite
in the afterlife?"

I discover sin-eaters,
medieval professionals who
consume bread and drink wine
off a dead person's coffin,
removing sins.

Meal at my father's headstone
would cleanse him
pure as a newborn.
But where are they today?

I recall Tet's Buddhist comments
about the power of belief and how
we shape our after-life.

I reach a solution:
in my heaven I believe my parents
will dwell together in peace
and love forever.

NOTES

1. *Issei* are first generation Japanese. They could not become US citizens until the 1950s. *Nisei* are second generation and are US citizens. *Sansei* are third generation U.S. citizens. The author is a *Sansei*.

2. In "Tess Calls Me a Shape Shifter"—Tess is Tess Gallagher. She is an internationally recognized poet and fiction writer, and widow of Raymond Carver, the late short story master referred to in the London Times as "America's Chekhov" at the time of his death.

3. In "Another Block 26 Photo"—the lines "When I grow up I want to be white. Being Japanese is too hard" is attributed to an unknown Japanese boy in camp—source unknown.

4. "Legacy" appears in *Glimpses of a Forever Foreigner*, CreateSpace, 2014.

5. "Unlike the Walrus and Carpenter" was written in celebration of the annual (2015) Walrus and Carpenter Picnic Event—Totten Inlet, Washington hosted by Taylor Shellfish and Jon Rowley with proceeds benefiting The Puget Sound Restoration Fund. The name of the event comes from Louis Carroll's poem of the same name where the walrus and carpenter trick a group of oysters into being eaten.

6. "La Medusa Cooking Class" was written in honor of the June 7th 2009 cooking class conducted by Chef Julie Andres at La Medusa Restaurant in Seattle.

   Menu: Aqua pazzo soup, fresh noodles with peas and morel mushrooms, and zabaglione.

   Wines: Stern Sauvignon Blanc, Domaine De Fonsainte "gris de Gris", and Malmsey Maderia.

7. "The Man from White River" was written in honor of the opening of the Hirabayashi Place residence, 310 Maynard Avenue South, Seattle 98104. The poem is on a plaque near the entrance. Hirabayashi resisted and challenged the WWII forced incarceration order of the Japanese up to the U.S. Supreme Court. Unfortunately, the Court ruled against him and the ruling stands today.

8. "Enola Gay and the Big Bomb" appears in *A Cold Wind from Idaho*, Black Lawrence Press, 2010, New York.

9. In "Actor's Studio" the line in French is a tip of the hat to Raymond Carver's title, *What We Talk About When We Talk About Love*, copyright 1974.

10. President Kennedy's quote is from Wikipedia. 1962. "Happy Birthday Mr. President."

11. "Just a Short Note to Say Something You Already Know" appears in *Take a Stand, Art Against Hate*, Raven Chronicles Press, 2020. The quote "History does not repeat itself, but it rhymes" is attributed to Mark Twain.

12. "Seeing Your Mother's Birthday Memorial Photos on Facebook" is about Erin whose mother died young from Multiple Systems Atrophy (MSA). Each year, Erin does numerous MSA fund raisers in her mother's memory.

ACKNOWLEDGEMENTS

Many thanks to my publisher, Jeanie Davies Okimoto, for her faith and hard work which turned the manuscript into a first class book. I'm indebted to Roger Shimomura for his cover art, "Kabuki Play", Alfredo Arreguin for "Portrait Larry Matsuda", and the late UW Professor Nelson Bentley who loved villanelles. I would like to thank Tess Gallagher for her unflagging support and assistance in proofing and critiquing "Shape Shifter: A Minidoka Concentration Camp Legacy."

Special thanks to my wife, Karen, for her love and support during my many hours of writing and proofing. Also thanks to Tilman Smith, Robyn Achilles, Anna Tamura, Carole Kubota, Dorothy Mann, Matthew & Jesika Matsuda, and A.C. Arai for their encouragement.

I want to acknowledge relatives and friends who were imprisoned at Minidoka and passed away: Ernest K. Matsuda, Hanae Matsuda, Alan Matsuda, Frank Kitamoto, Louise Kashino, Peggy Mitchell, Shizuko & Dr. Hajime Mitsumori, Kenjiro & Elsie Yamada, Toyo-jiro & Toku Yamada, Koko & Ed Matsuda, May Namba, Shigeo & Toshiko Yabusaki, Koemon & Sumi Matsuda, Mary Matsuda Gruenewald, Min Masuda, Kaz and Kiku Tatsumi, Fumi Numoto, and Yoshitada (Yosh) Nakagawa.

Also I want to recognize my friends and relatives who supported me through the years: Vivian Lee & the late Owen Lee, Gregory Piercy & the late Sue Tomita, Mark Johnson & the late Carol Benge, Carol Simmons & the late Jimmie Simmons, Brad, Allison, & Stella Joseph, Gary & Carrie Dodobara, Wendy Lustbader & Barry Grosskopf, Annie & Bill Becker, Alfredo Arreguin & Susie Lytle, Mandy Dixon Kuehmichel, Joe Okimoto, Jane & Larry Briscoe, Binko & John Bisbee, Tilman Smith & Michael Nailen, Lynn & Jay Arakaki, June Kamigawachi & Mark Mansuri, Vivi, Melissa, & Evelyn Matsuda, Pam & Daniel Krute, A.C. & Jerry

Arai, Linda Ando, Lauren Iida, Volly Iida, Erin Shigaki, Charles Wright, Jay & Raku Rubin, Jean Nakayama, Karen Maeda Allman, Rick Simonson, Erin Williams, Francine Seders, John & Polly Shigaki, Gina & Jerry Corso, Tets Kashima, A. Barretto Ogilvie, Frank & Felicita Irigon, Ellen & John Gordon Hill, Terrance Rabbitt, Cassie Chinn, Steve Sumida & Gail Nomura, Assunta Ng, Wayne Nakanishi & Carol Roxborough, Dwight & Cynthia Imanaka, Jeff & Pam Kawaguchi, Henry & Garbo Chin, Tim Tsubahara, Tom Yamada, Tomio Moriguchi, Mustey Shiga, Don Gillmore, Satsuki Ina, Amy Sahm, and Lainey Terada Sahm.

Also thanks to organizations: The Friends of Minidoka, Raven Chronicles, Mukai Foundation, Minidoka Pilgrimage, Nisei Veterans' Committee Foundation, and Wing Luke Museum.

Thanks to more friends: Michelle Kumata, Jason & Mizuho Rabbitt Tomita, Alan & Joyce Rudolph, Ben Pederson, Carol Nygren, Paul Murakami, Grant & Linda Kunishige, Yuri Kinoshita, Jay MacGregor & Kyoko Maeda, Willon & Arlene Lew, George & Nancy Fujimoto, Eugene Tagawa, Arlene & Ed Hee, Patty & Oliver Pickford, Connie Toda, Grace Mitchell, Carol Schroeder, Ida Jane Mitsumori, Phoebe Bosche, Anna Balint, Etsuko Ichikawa, Evelyn Finklea, Jane DeHaan, Ken Mayeda & Eliane Dao, Peg Cheng & Marcus Donner, Rory Banyard, Debbie Kashino, Bruce Inaba, Katsuya & Harumi Endo, Matt Sasaki, May Sasaki, Jan Johnson, Ken & Ann Yabusaki, Eric Banh & Teresa Nguyen, Elaine Ikoma Ko, Dorrine Zelmer, David Yamaguchi, Gary Copeland Lilley, Tracey Paine, Rose Masters, Mary Jane Fraser, Amy Astle-Raaen, Jeremy Raaen, Isabel Raaen, Violet Raaen, Julie Andres, Andrea Johansen, Mia Russell, Hanako Wakasuka-Chong, Rick Tanigawa, Matt Dillon, Wendy Tokuda, Barb Lui & the late Kip Tokuda, Rita Brogan, and Lois Fleming.

Finally, I want to recognize friends who passed away who are not listed above: Andy Shiga, Robert Sims, John Rowley, Reverend Mineo Katagiri, Phil Hayasaka, Cookie, Shoji Suko, Harry Lawson,

Deborah Knutson, Tom Sheehan, Don Kinsley, Harry & Michi Sakohira, Isao Nishimura, Henry & Chiyeko Yamada, Josie Gray, Reverend Lincoln Eng, John Humphries, Sam Kelly, Bill Hilliard, Mike Castillano, Don Kazama, and Alan Sugiyama.

Lawrence Matsuda was born in the Minidoka, Idaho Concentration Camp during World War II. He and his family were among the approximately 120,000 Japanese Americans and Japanese held without due process for approximately three years or more. Matsuda has a Ph.D. in education from the University of Washington and was: a Seattle Schools secondary teacher, UW university counselor, state level administrator, Seattle school principal, Seattle assistant superintendent, educational consultant, visiting professor at Seattle University (SU), and school design consultant. Currently he is a poet and author.

In 2005, he and two Seattle University colleagues co-edited the book, *Community and Difference:Teaching, Pluralism and Social Justice*, Peter Lang Publishing, New York. It won the 2006 National Association of Multicultural Education Phillip Chinn Book Award. In July of 2010, his book of poetry entitled, *A Cold Wind from Idaho*, about the WWII forced incarceration of Japanese Americans was published by Black Lawrence Press in New York. In August of 2014 his book of poetry, *Glimpses of a Forever Foreigner*, was released. It is collaboration between Matsuda and artist Roger Shimomura who contributed 17 original sketches.

In 2015, Matsuda collaborated with artist, Matt Sasaki, and produced a graphic novel: *An American Hero-Shiro Kashino* (stand-alone chapter) which is Chapter One of *Fighting for America: Nisei Soldiers*. The Shiro Kashino animated video won a 2015 regional Emmy. In 2016, he and Tess Gallagher collaborated on *Boogie Woogie CrissCross* a book of poetry developed from e-mails they exchanged over a period of three years where she was in Ireland and he was in Seattle. It was published by MadHat Press.

In 2016, chapter two of his graphic novel, *An American Hero: Frank Nishimura*, was nominated for two Regional Emmys and won one for best editing.

In 2019, his novel based on his mother's experience entitled, *My Name Is Not Viola* (Endicott and Hugh Books) was released. She was born in Seattle, educated in Japan, returned to Seattle and married, evacuated during WWII, had two children in camp, was institutionalized in the 1950s and was released to live a productive life.

Currently, Matsuda is writing two separate biographies, *The Life and Times of Andy Shiga* and a book about Harry Sotaro Kawabe.